D0585538

Hats and Bonnets

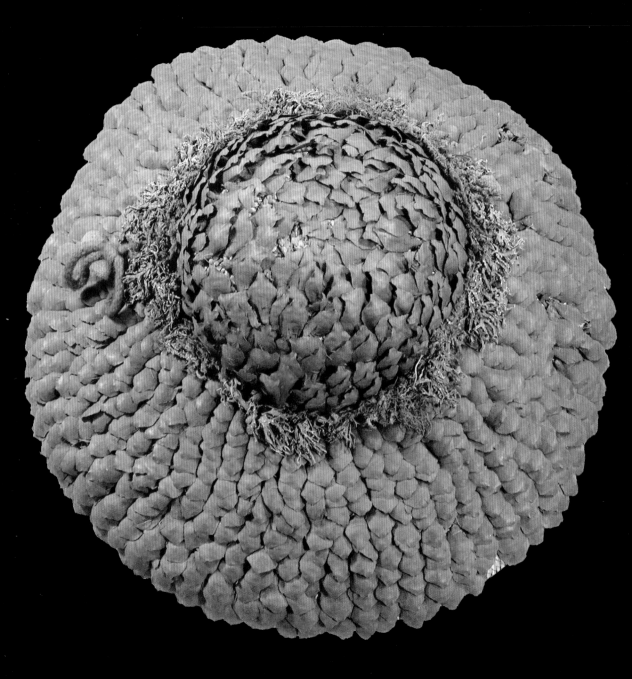

Hats and Bonnets

by Althea Mackenzie

Special Photography by Richard Blakey

THE NATIONAL TRUST

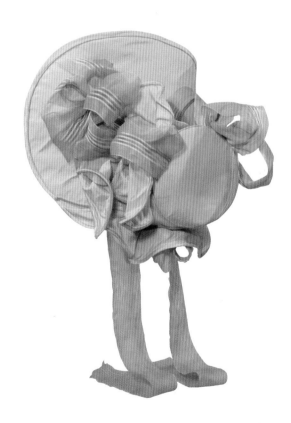

Introduction

The Wade Collection is not only one of the major collections of costume owned by the National Trust, but also represents a private collection of world-class quality.

Its creator, Charles Paget Wade, was born in 1883. His father was part-owner of a family sugar plantation in St Kitts so that he was brought up in comfortable circumstances, although his childhood with his grandmother in Great Yarmouth in Norfolk was spartan. An instinct for collecting was acquired early, along with a strong sense of place and heritage.

However, the world around him was rapidly changing, compounded by the social, political and economic impact of the First World War. For Wade, this meant that much of what he had relied on as a valuable reference was being destroyed by a society that looked away from the past, and forward to a notion of progress based on material wealth and mass production. Traditional modes and mores were seen as unsustainable and undesirable.

Wade's response was to begin collecting objects that reflected man's craftsmanship and ingenuity. This was very much in tune with the ideals and beliefs of exponents of the Arts & Crafts Movement, such as the architects M.H. Baillie Scott and Sir Edwin Lutyens. In 1919 he bought Snowshill, a derelict but largely unspoilt Cotswold manor, and set about restoring the house and garden drawing on the fundamental principles of Arts & Crafts.

The manor house at Snowshill was the repository for his collections, which covered an astonishing range, from scientific instruments to samurai armour, from cabinets to clocks, from bicycles to kitchen bygones. Wade himself lived in the next door priest's house, to give over maximum space to the objects. In 1948 he decided to hand over his house, gardens and collections to the National Trust. James Lees-Milne, who was responsible for negotiating the transfer of historic houses to the care of the Trust, found Wade the most eccentric of all the owners he had to deal with – no mean feat in a contest replete with eccentric contenders.

In his diary, Lees-Milne drew a vivid pen portrait of Wade: 'Wearing square-cut, shoulder-length, Roundhead hair and dressed in trunk and hose, this magpie collector would, while showing visitors over the house, suddenly disappear behind a tapestry panel to emerge through a secret door on a different level.'

Wade was, in fact, wearing some examples from his magnificent costume collection. This consists of over 2,200 items, the majority dating from the 18th and 19th centuries, many unique and most of astounding quality. Geographically the collection incorporates material from diverse cultures; for example, from Africa, Russia and the Middle East. Historically it provides a comprehensive record of changing fashions before the impact of uniformity brought about by the effects of industrial revolution and mass production. The range is vast: 18th- and 19th-century dresses (many unaltered), complete men's suits from the 18th century, beautifully embroidered 18th- and 19th-century men's waistcoats, military uniforms, servants' clothes, ecclesiastical costume, accessories such as hats and shoes. The collection is unusual in that Wade valued the utilitarian and mundane as well as the rare and precious.

Originally Wade kept the costume collection in cupboards, drawers and on display in Occidens, a room so named to evoke associations of the West and the setting sun. The clothes also provided an authentic wardrobe for some of the amateur dramatics that were performed at Snowshill, with friends such as John Betjeman, J.B.Priestley, Lutyens and Virginia Woolf. He intended that a special gallery should be built, but the plan was abandoned with the outbreak of the Second World War. On behalf of the National Trust, the collection was looked after and catalogued by the costume historian Nancy Bradfield, and subsequently by the Trust's own conservators at their studio at Blickling Hall in Norfolk.

Now, while all the other collections remain at Snowshill, the costumes and accessories are housed at Berrington Hall in Herefordshire. Because of the constraints of space, it is primarily a reserve collection available for viewing by appointment. The vulnerability innate in costume restricts display opportunities, although portions of the collection are regularly on display at Snowshill and at Berrington. However, access is vital, and this volume, the first of a series illustrated with specially commissioned photographs, is one way of enabling readers world-wide to enjoy such an important collection.

The selection of women's hats and bonnets from Charles Paget Wade's costume collection covers the period from the 18th century to the end of the 19th century. As with other areas of his amazing bequest to the National Trust, he applied strict criteria that underpinned all his collecting. Simply put, these criteria were 'design, colour and craftsmanship' which he combined with a

passion for preserving and restoring examples of social history that were in danger of being lost forever.

Although just one aspect of the costume collection, the hats, bonnets and caps represent a comprehensive journey through the fashions of a period that saw major and radical social changes taking place such as the French Revolution, the industrial revolution, and the emancipation of women. In the 18th century, as in earlier centuries, women of every level of society would have worn a hat, bonnet or cap at all times during the day, whether indoors or out. These not only performed the function of providing warmth and tidiness and, for some, modesty, but they also became an avenue for style and fashion statements.

A head covering also served as a gauge for the values of society. The confidence and prosperity of the mid-18th century is reflected in the bizarre range and excesses of headwear and hairstyles, whereas the concepts of liberty and fraternity introduced by the French Revolution resulted in an adoption of 'lower class' forms of dress. Hats also served to mark specific events like marriage and mourning, as well as identifying membership of a particular group, such as the Quaker Society of Friends.

The distinction between hats and bonnets is somewhat blurred but a bonnet is generally defined as headwear that ties under the chin whilst a hat generally has a shaped crown and brim.

I would like to thank Clare Bowyer who has helped me to assemble the hats and begin the research on them, Richard Blakey for his patience and skill in taking the photographs, Stuart Smith for his designer's artistic eye, and Margaret Willes, my publisher, for coordinating all the disparate elements, of which there have been many.

Lastly I am grateful to the staff at Berrington Hall and Snowshill Manor for their support.

Althea Mackenzie
Curator of the Wade Costume Collection

Bergère 1750s

Portrait of Lady Henrietta Herbert by Sir Joshua Reynolds, c.1777, from Powis Castle, Powys. She is wearing a very large bergère, veering towards the breakfast table.

The earliest hats in the Snowshill Collection come from the mid-18th century, when the fashion and social behaviour of the aristocracy in France and England reached heights of excess. These extremes were characterised at the French Court by the Pompadour style, named after Louis XV's mistress, Madame de Pompadour, and lampooned mercilessly in contemporary caricatures.

The height to which the hair, real and false, rose and the ingenuity to which the decoration could aspire created a significant role for the hair-dresser. One such from Siberia advertised in 1770 his ability to 'make any lady's head appear like the head of a lion, wolf, tiger, bear, fox, peacock, swan, goose, Friesland hen or any other bird'.

But for milliners these developments provided a challenge. One of the most versatile and popular styles to develop was the round, low-crowned hat that could perch at any angle on the top of any amount of hair. Size varied from the plain round 'mushroom-shaped' hat such as the one shown here to 'hats remarkable large: some as large as the smallest sized round breakfast tables' according to *Gentleman's and London Magazine* or *Monthly Chronologer* of 1777.

This perfectly round hat, made from straw wound in a spiral closely stitched with thick linen thread is 30cms/11½ ins in diameter. It is of a flat conical shape with a very small, flattened point at the crown. The lining is of claret silk taffeta and it is edged with very narrow plaited straw braid. The ties are of wide matching claret ribbon, attached beneath the crown with a ribbon rosette on each of the ties.

6

Bergère 1730-70

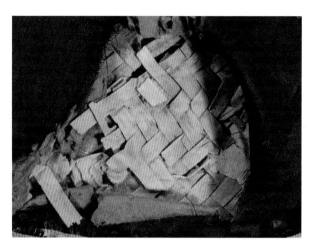

Bergère hats from Edward Smith's Angling Party *painted in 1773, now at Wimpole Hall in Cambridgeshire.*

A typical example of a bergère, if somewhat more crudely made than the hat on pp.6 and 7. It is constructed of plaited chip made from fine slivers of wood that offered a cheaper alternative to straw. The chip is covered with fawn paper and a layer of blue-black silk. The underside is lined with cream paper and cream silk gauze. Blue-mauve and cream box-pleated striped ribbon trims the brim, forming puffs around the top and bottom of the crown. These extend into ties which are looped to form a false bow when attached with a flattened brass hook and steel eye.

The brim edge is bound by black velvet ribbon. The black machine-made lace under the brim is a later addition: machine-made lace was not widely available until after the patenting of John Heathcoat's bobbin net machine in 1809 (see p.72).

8

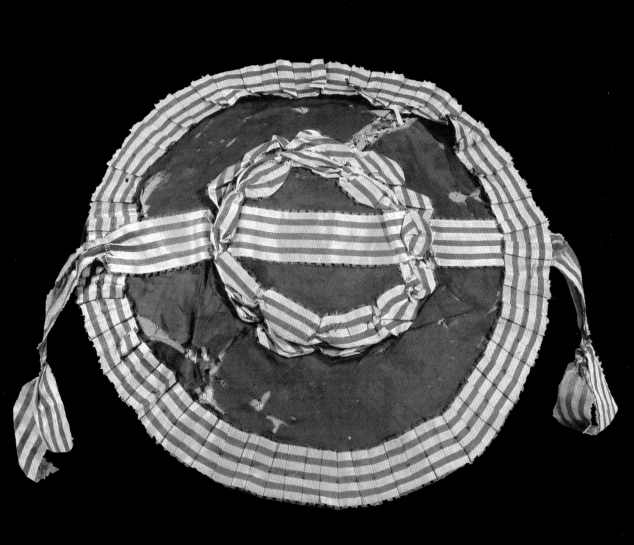

Bergère 1750s

An 18th-century milkmaid wearing her bergère from an engraving by Shepherd after H.W.Bunbury.

The bergère had traditionally been associated with older women and servant girls, but in the 18th century came to be associated with an increase in countryside pursuits. This style of hat, variously known as the shepherdess, milkmaid or bergère, persisted as a fashion throughout the century. In 1727 Charles de Saussure, a Swiss traveller to Britain, commented on this trend for 'small hats of straw that are vastly becoming. Ladies even of the highest rank are thus attired when they go walking or make a simple visit.'

This hat of modest proportions is constructed with whole straw twisted around a central core. The straw is overlapped closely to make a thick fabric that has then been covered with thick fawn paint and varnished to give further body and a degree of waterproofing. The underside is covered with a chocolate-brown printed cotton decorated with a small leaf spot print in grey and red. There is a small, shallow false crown and a medium-sized brim that turns down all round. Seven wooden plates stitched beneath the rim stiffen and add weight to the construction.

The hat is trimmed with a narrow band of matching decorative plait. The wide cream, blue and pink checked silk ribbon ties are a later addition.

Bergère 1750-1770

This is a large, round, flat-brimmed, shallow-crowned hat made from a split straw plait, the straw being a combination of natural and dyed to create a checkered effect. The hat is lined with old rose silk with a stamped design of zigzags and ripples. A band of fancy plait decorates the inside of the brim and a garland of split straw cord and tassels decorate the crown.

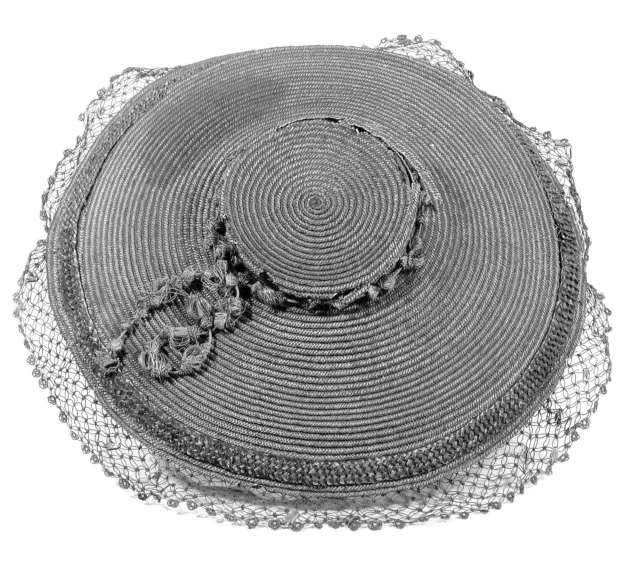

Cap Mid-18th century

Mary Anne de la Pole with her brothers from a portrait by Thomas Beach painted in 1793, now at Antony House in Cornwall. She is wearing an ornate indoor cap decorated with ribbon, and holds her straw hat.

Caps were an integral part of dress throughout the 18th and 19th centuries. They were worn at all times of day resulting in great variation in style – whether for indoor wear, for undress (informal occasions), for dress (formal occasions) or for outdoor wear. Bernard Lens in *The Exact Dress of the Head*, published in 1725, commented on the increasing variety of head-dress. The styles were often named after their shape – the Dormeuse (Dormouse), the Fly or the Butterfly. They could also be named after the type of lace from which they were made – blonde, Brussels or Bugle. As hairstyles and hats changed, so did the caps. They

were, for instance, worn under the bergère hats shown on pp. 7 to 13.

This indoor cap is one of the more functional and practical examples from the 18th-century period. It is made from a fine linen and has been exquisitely decorated with Queen Anne quilting in yellow silk backstitch. The construction is of four sections that fit closely over the head and ears. The beautiful natural design flows over the cap with carnations, leaves and buds surrounded by a vermicular ground.

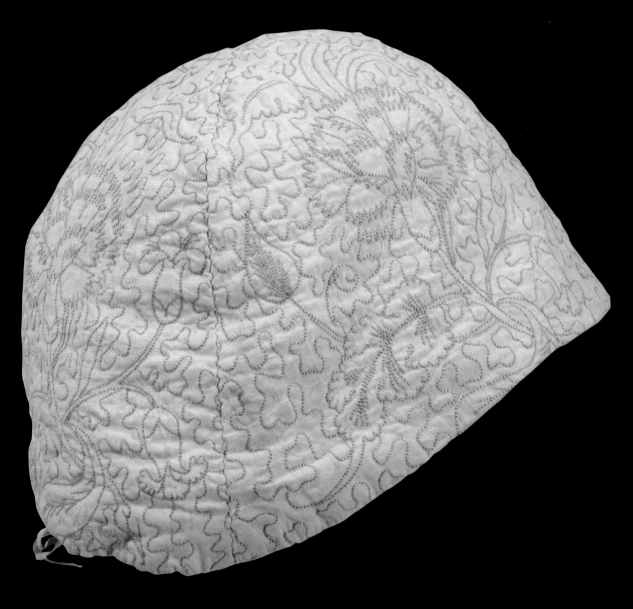

Calashes 1770-1810

Pin print showing a lady of fashion of the early 1780s wearing a very stylish calash.

A more practical head-covering was the calash or calèche that provided outdoor protection for the head, or head and hat combined. Deriving its name from the 17th-century light carriage with a collapsing hood, the calash was similarly a collapsible construction made from whalebone or cane hoops covered with fabric. The size varied as much as the hairstyles and headwear.

For an increasingly country-loving society, it was universally adopted because of its great practicality. It could, for instance, be waterproofed for walking parties. The *London Magazine* of 1772 explained 'as with a ribbon pulled it can entirely cover the face by which means it is preserved from the sun. It serves instead of a hat and does not require the hair to be dressed.' Five years later, *The Gentleman's and London Magazine* or *Monthly Chronologer* observed less flatteringly that the calash provided opportunity for 'our young misses and old maids still [to] continue to bury their empty heads…'.

These calashes are of modest proportions in comparison to many of the period. The example on the right is made from sable-brown glazed cotton supported by seven cane hoops and lined with baby-pink glazed cotton. It has a short, lined curtain and is pleated in a ring centre-back with a central self-covered card 'button'.

There is a brown silk ribbon draw-tie at the back with a wider brown ribbon loop attached to top of the front edge for holding the calash extended. The calash came into Charles Wade's collection with a handwritten label attached 'Calash (c.1805) worn by Mrs J W Lavender of Evesham.'

The calash shown above is of nutmeg-brown glazed cotton formed over six split cane hoops. It has a fawn silk ribbon loop at the centre-front for holding the calash extended when in use.

16

Hoods 19th century

This detail from an engraving by Wenceslaus Hollar dates from the 1640s, but the hood worn by a lady representing 'Winter' is very similar in style to the examples on these pages. Hoods were practical pieces of headwear and not greatly susceptible to changes in fashion.

The hood performed a similar function to the calash. The far right example, dating from the early 19th century, is made from black silk lined with royal blue silk quilted in a diamond pattern. It is gathered into a narrow strip along the top of the head, drawn up along the lower edge to give a short curtain hiding the face. It is fastened with black silk ribbon drawstring and ties centre-back.

The second hood, right, dates from the mid-19th century. The black silk is quilted in a diamond pattern and trimmed with a wide coral-pink, box-pleated ribbon trim.

Poke Bonnets 1815-30

Poke bonnets were worn with delicate, clinging muslin dresses which were frequently satirised in caricatures. This detail is from a caricature by George Cruikshank published in 1803, where Jack Frost is pursuing ladies dressed in fashionable but impractical costumes.

The period of social confusion after the French Revolution brought about a radical change in attitude to fashion. The emphasis shifted from ostentatious display of wealth and status to a classical simplicity where the desired qualities were purity and grace. For a short period an apparent modesty entered into fashion.

In terms of headwear, the hat was no longer the dominant form, being relegated to the role of providing protection from the sun or rain when pursuing increasingly popular outdoor activities such as walking and riding. The style for hair was cropped and face-framing, with headwear emulating an idealistic if rather inaccurate notion of the classical profile. The result was the poke bonnet. These tended to be rigid in form, decorated with ribbons and tied under the chin. The bonnets shown here and on pp.22-3 are three fine examples and give credence to the observation in *The Hermit in London*, 1819, that ' the poke of her bonnet only allowed her countenance to be seen in perspective'.

The first example, dating from *c.* 1815, is made from a 3-end plait with a matt appearance. The plait is hand-stitched with interlocking stitches through overlapping plaits. It is fully lined with a white dotted, peony-red cotton with edges and ties of black cotton tape.

The second example dates from the 1820s. It, too, is of 3-end plait with a matt appearance. It has an oval crown, vertical at the back of the head and stepped into the neck. The straight line across the top of the head frames the face to cheek level. The lining is of glazed cotton with a roller- and block-printed, floral striped design and is edged with blue silk ribbon with cotton tape ties pinned to the bonnet for fastening.

20

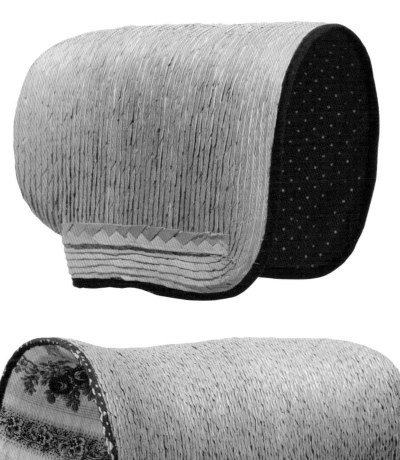

Poke Bonnet 1815-20

This example is made from narrow shiny straw plait. The shiny appearance of a plait was determined by the nature of the straw (rice, wheat, etc) or whether the outer or inner surface of the straw was uppermost in the plait. The bonnet is lined with a steel blue silk over an interlining of paper. The crown forms a straight line across the top of the head while the flat vertical crown steps into the back of the neck, the whole forming a narrow frame for the face. It is hand-stitched with small random stitches through the overlapped plait making the form very stiff. A very fine horsehair and straw braid edges the brim.

Ties of blue and cream flowered ribbon also form the decoration to the sides of the bonnet and under the crown.

Poke bonnets were not to everybody's taste. The *Ipswich Journal* in June 1799 commented 'The ladies have just now adopted a repulsive kind of hat which may be called the Poking hat: it has a long projection like the beak of a snipe, and is a good guard against all familiar approaches of those who have any regard for their eyes.'

Plaits

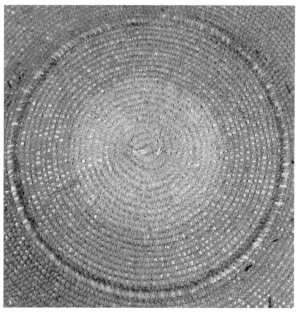

The growing importance of straw for the production of fashionable hats is reflected in the huge increase of imports of leghorn both in the form of hats and as a raw material. Leghorn straw, *Tritium Turgidum*, from Legorno, now Livorno, in Tuscany, was considered the premium straw for hat manufacture. By 1760 over one and half a million hats were being imported. The American War of Independence and the revolutionary wars with France, however, seriously disrupted the trade to Britain and led to the Royal Society of Arts in London encouraging the search for straws that could be produced locally. Various alternatives were eventually found, leading to thriving home industries in the Midlands, Bedfordshire and Hertfordshire. Plait schools were set up where children as young as three would be taught the intricacies of straw plaiting in return for a generally meagre education.

Top row, left to right:
Straw wound in a spiral and closely stitched with thick linen thread (bergère, mid-18th century, pp.6-7)
3-end straw plait overlapped (poke bonnet, 1820s, pp.20-1)
13-end straw plait overlapped and hand-stitched (bonnet, 1840s)
Bottom row, left to right:
7-end straw plait, overlapped and hand-stitched (bonnet, late 1830s, early '40s, pp.32-3)
Leghorn straw plait woven in one piece from the centre (bonnet, 1815-20, pp.22-3)

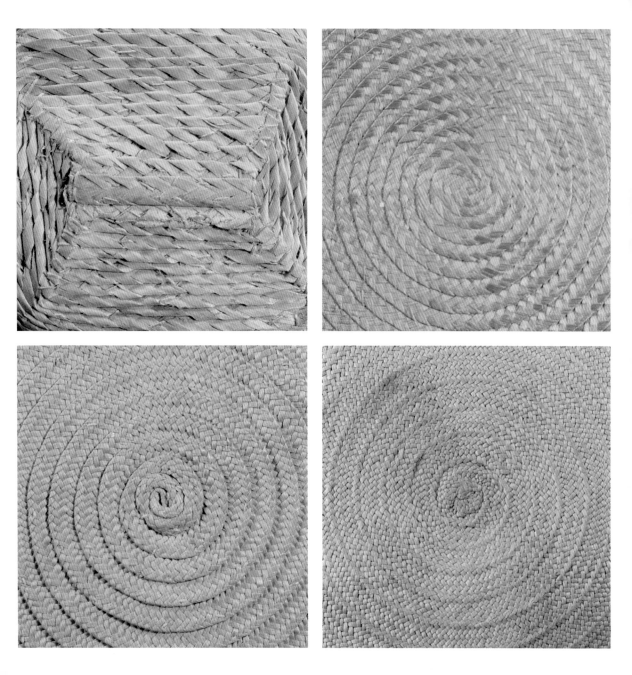

Bonnet Late 1820s

French fashion plate showing bonnets from the late 1820s.

The end of the Napoleonic Wars in 1815 enabled a resumption of relations between Britain and France. Influenced by French fashion, an exuberance returned to dress styles. Large bonnets were worn on all occasions with dresses that had exaggerated gigot sleeves, tightly laced waists and wide, shorter skirts. Formal bonnets were commonly made from silk satin, often stiffened with whalebone and decorated lavishly with silk gauze – one of the most desirable and expensive of available trimmings. The French town St Etienne, a major producer of ribbons during this period, employed in the region of 100,000 people producing an ever-increasing range of exquisite trimmings in silk, satin and velvet. During this period there was a change in hairstyles, which moved away from close-cropped, classically inspired styles to those based on curls that framed the face.

This beautiful bonnet of ivory silk is a particularly fine example of an evening bonnet. The silk covers stiffened linen muslin with edges reinforced with wire and bands of plaited straw. It has a very deep and widening brim with a deep, straight-sided crown, sloped top and upturned bavolet. The bavolet, forming a curtain at the back, became a characteristic of the bonnet form for the next few decades.

The lining of the brim is of matching ivory silk and the bonnet is trimmed with two large wings of silk with wired edges and large bows of Cambridge blue silk gauze ribbons. Loops are held in place with narrow, blue-wired ribbon that also trims the inside of the brim. The trimmings are pinned in place.

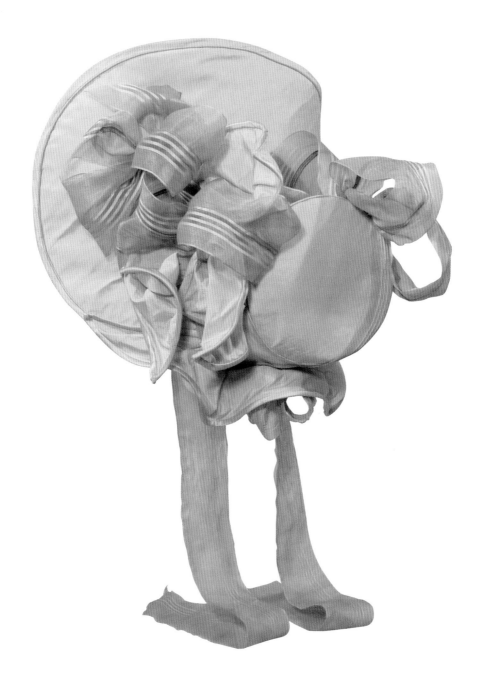

Leghorn Bonnet 1830-35

Detail from At the Shoemaker's, *painted by an unknown artist in the 1820s. The bonnet on the left is very like the example shown on pp. 26 and 27. The hat on the right is what was derogatorily known as a chimney-pot hat.*

Despite the efforts made to boost home industries in Britain, leghorn continued to be the most desirable straw for plaiting. The *Manchester Iris* in 1823 reported 'It appears by a return made to parliament that in the year ending April 5 1823 there were 136,045 leghorn straw hats imported into Great Britain and 3,312 lbs of straw plaiting.'

This example is characteristic of the large bonnets worn outdoors. As with poke bonnets, the style was open to satire and ridicule. One English commentator on French fashion remarked 'The ugliest part of their habiliments is the high chimneys on their heads.'

It is woven in one piece from the centre of the crown, a technique typical of the leghorn bonnet. The brim is very deep, widening with a sharp angle between it and the crown, which is deep sided with a domed top. The brim is wire edged. There is no lining but remains of a paper lining stuck inside the crown with '44' pencilled on the side.

The headband and tie, which are later additions, are of cream ribbed silk with small brocaded flower motifs. A green ribbon beneath a band of ruched cream chiffon decorates the brim, probably also a later addition.

Winter Bonnet 1830-40

This bonnet is made from woven willow chip (see p.8). It is covered with novelty fabric – a purple-brown cotton ground decorated with loops of garnet silk fringing woven in to give a fluffy appearance. The colour suggests it is a winter bonnet. It again has a deep wide brim and deep straight-sided crown at a shallow angle to the brim. The crown edge is piped with pansy satin at the join of the brim and crown on the outside, and the brim is lined with cream satin and edged with wire.

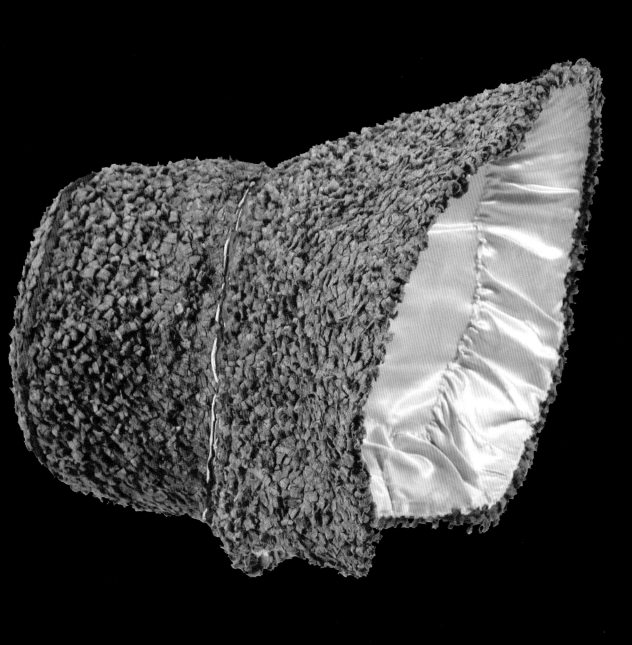

Bonnet Late 1830s - 40s

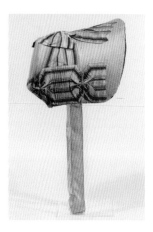

When Queen Victoria ascended the throne in 1837 at the age of eighteen, she became associated with femininity and respectability displayed through dress and demeanour. Writing twenty years later to her son the Prince of Wales (the future Edward VII) she suggested that dress 'gives also the one outward sign from which people in general can and often do judge upon the inward state of mind and feeling of a person'. She continued 'we do not wish to control your own tastes and fancies ... but we do expect, that you will never wear anything extravagant or slang'.

The close-fitting bonnet was perfect for the typical bun with side ringlets that Victoria made so popular (see p.36). The bonnet became universal for the following decade, changing little in shape. The preferred style had a crown and brim that merged to a single horizontal line. The sides of the brim curved down over the ears forming a low oval frame to the face. The bonnet strings emerged from inside the brim to be tied under the chin, eventually attaching to the brim itself. The bavolet continued to be a significant feature, as did the emphasis on the lining and the decoration of the inner edging.

This straw bonnet is made from 7-end plaited straw, overlapped and hand-stitched. The crown tilts upwards at the back and the brim tilts upwards at the front with a straight lower edge. This serves to hide the profile. It is shaped with rough card with a double row of wire at the brim. There is another layer of different plaited straw between the outer layer and card on the brim, possibly just at the brim edge only.

The trimmings are of wide silk ribbon with coloured ribbed stripes making a band with a large bow over the top of the crown and brim. It is pleated and ruched around the lower edge and pinned into position. A fawn silk ribbon makes a semicircle for the tie.

Trimmings

During the 19th century the production of plaits continued to be very much a rural home-based industry whilst millinery gradually became an urban profession, often carried out in association with dressmaking. A wide variety of affordable trimmings also became available to a greater number of people in the mid-century. Ribbons, lace and the machine-made bobbin net laces and appliquéed nets offered great scope for adaptation and renewal of trimmings for those who had the money and time on their hands.

In *Pride and Prejudice* Jane Austen has Lydia Bennett declaring 'Look here, I have bought this bonnet, I do not think it is very pretty; but I thought I might as well buy it as not. I shall pull it to pieces as soon as I get home, and see if I can make it up any better … . I have bought some prettier-coloured satin to trim it with fresh, I think it will be very tolerable.'

Silk ribbons, top row left to right:
Grey and green brocade (bonnet, 1850s, p.54)
Blue and cream flowered ribbon (poke bonnet, 1815-20, pp.22 and 23)
Blue-mauve and cream striped ribbon (bergère, 1730-70, pp. 8 and 9)
Bottom row, left to right:
Maroon ribbon with yellow and black scalloped edging (bonnet, 1840s, p.45)
Maroon ribbon (bonnet, 1840s, p.43)

Bonnet 1840s

Fancy braids of great intricacy were very much the fashion at this period, often made from straw plaiting, horsehair, or a combination of both.

This bonnet is made from horsehair, cotton and straw alternating with black and cream straw mesh. The bonnet forms a straight line from the crown to the brim, slanting upwards to the front. The sides curve down to points under the chin and the back is decorated with a ribbon bavolet edged with narrow straw braid. The brim is edged with wire. The crown has a side lining of black silk and the brim of ruched lapis lazuli blue silk ribbon joined to form a fabric.

The whole is trimmed with blue ribbon across the top. A bunch of brown leaves and buds decorate the centre front. There is a ribbon low centre back and the bonnet is fastened with narrow blue ribbon ties.

This style of bonnet complemented the fashionable female coiffure at this period. In terms of female coiffure this meant a move from the exaggerated top-knot and elaborate curls to a sleeker, flat-topped arrangement. In 'How to Arrange the Hair' written by a member of the Ladies Committee of Almacks, the social arbiters of the day, it is noted that by 1857 'hair has been for a long period worn

Madonna like, drawn plain over each cheek like the Queen'. This continued to be fashionable until the Queen's influence on fashion declined after the death of Prince Albert in 1861.

Plain Caps 19th century

Caps continued to be worn indoors in the morning and for informal occasions. Variations were great but gradually caps became much smaller and by the 1850s, for many young women, alternatives were found in the form of decorative ribbons and lace. One commentator advised 'young married ladies do not wear caps until they acquire the endearing name of "Mother"'.

Lace ribbons and starched frills were often employed to trim indoor caps, forming a 'halo' around the face.

The first example, above, dating from the 1830s, is of white dimity with a small round crown, high at the back of the head. The white muslin frills would probably have been crimped.

The second cap, right, dates from the mid-19th century. It is made of white cotton trimmed with muslin frills and two hand-worked bands of *broderie anglaise* insertions.

Fancy Caps 19th century

Portrait of Dorothy Whitmore-Jones by E.V. Rippingille, 1850, at Chastleton House, Oxfordshire. The sitter is wearing a fancy cap in fine lace.

Fancy caps were worn on more formal occasions, such as evening entertainments.

The first example above, dating from c.1850, is of white muslin with a fine example of Heathcoat's 3-twist bobbin net (see p.72) with a machine-run spot motif. There are two rows of Valenciennes lace around the brim, and cream satin ribbon edging the top brim.

The second cap, right, is of stiffened machine-cotton net. It has a wide brim with rounded points over the ears and is tied under the chin. The face is framed with a double frill of silk net lace and ribbon, and the edge is stiffened with heavy net. It is trimmed with rows of lupin-blue china ribbon and wider lilac ribbon across the back, and is tied with lilac ribbon.

Bonnets 1840s

The first bonnet, right, is made in burgundy wool and silk, with a soft round crown gathered at the back of the neck with a crown that slants in a straight line to the brim edge. The sides curve down to points under the chin and the back is decorated with a bavolet. The satin brim is ruched onto four rows of wire with bands of cloth over gathering stitches. The bonnet is lined with cream silk with a frill of silk tulle edged with blonde lace on a silk-covered straw plait frame inside the brim. There is matching red feather decoration over the crown and along the sides of the bonnet, with wide maroon silk ribbons hanging from the points and narrow cream ribbon ties.

The second bonnet, far right, is made from purple-brown silk velvet with a lining of cream silk stamped with the maker's name 'MISS LINCOLN, milliner, Broad Row, Yarmouth'. The fabric covers stiffened leno of different weights and stiffness and the brim is edged with cane. The bonnet is decorated with tubes of velvet stiffened with wire with small ostrich plumes dyed to match. A garland of silk tulle is edged with blonde lace, moss rosebuds of cream and pink cotton and pressed and painted cotton leaves on wire.

The decoration of the inner edging of bonnets with artificial flowers, lace and other trimmings, forming a frame for the face, was very much a feature of this period. Mrs M.J.Howell in her *Handbook of Millinery* published in 1847 pronounced: 'no one article in the whole range of female costume is more important in its effects than the comparatively small piece of satin, silk or other material that forms the lining of the bonnet'.

Bonnet 1840s

Detail from an English fashion plate, December 1841.

A fine example of a bonnet of straw plait with alternating fancy straw braid. It has scalloped edges and a maroon silk bavolet lined with cream silk. It is hand-stitched through overlapped plait and braid. The back edge is reinforced and the edge of the brim caned. Three strips of maroon velvet, one with a punched scalloped edge and holes, trims the bonnet and two wide punched velvet pieces hang at the right-hand side. The crown is lined with cream silk drawn up with a running thread over cotton wadding. The brim is lined with dawn-pink taffeta ruched over three rows of cane and has a garland of pink and maroon pressed-velvet petals and silk tulle on a wire frame pinned inside the brim.

The bonnet fastens with wide maroon silk ribbons with yellow and black scalloped edging which hang from the points of the brim.

44

Fancy Braids & Weaves

By the middle of the 19th century, ornate braids were generally available. Milliners would acquire plaited straw from plait schools, from Italy and from sources further afield, such as China, and then add further decoration, often a combination of horsehair and straw.

Top row, left to right:
Two details from bonnet, 1840s (pp. 36 and 37)
Detail from bonnet, 1840s (p.45)
Bottom row, left to right:
Detail from bonnet, 1840s (p.45)
Detail of fancy horsehair, bonnet, 1885-90 (p.87)

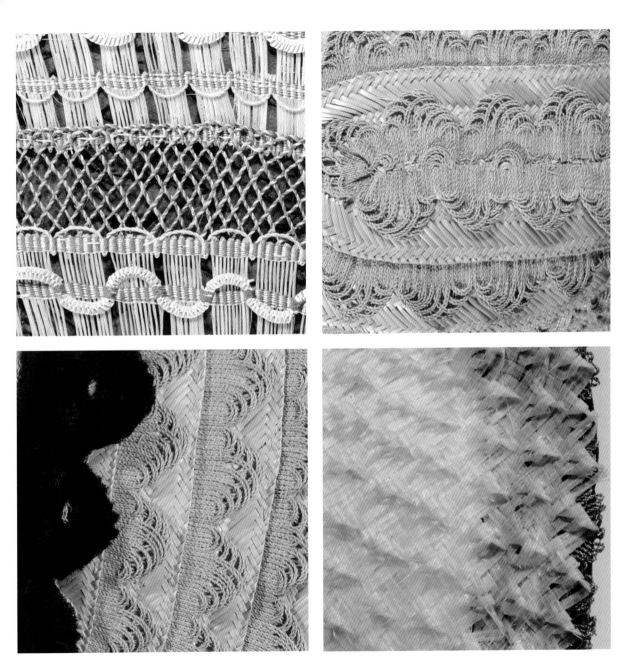

Mourning Bonnet 1840

Detail from Dividend Day at the Bank of England, *painted by George Elgar Hicks in 1859 and now at Wimpole Hall in Cambridgeshire. The lady on the right is wearing mourning dress and bonnet.*

During the Victorian period, the etiquette of mourning became very formalised. Black was the universally accepted colour for the first phase, full mourning. A woman might swathe herself in black crape and veiling for two years after the death of her husband and for a year following the death of a close member of the family. Subsequent stages were marked by wearing half-mourning, when shades of grey, lilac and mauve were acceptable.

This mourning bonnet is of black ciré (glazed, shiny silk) over a sized muslin form with heavier stiffening to the brim that is also edged with wire. The brim is self-lined and the crown lined with black silk. The deep crown tilts slightly upwards with a deep brim widening slightly towards the front. It has a deep bavolet. The bonnet hides most of the profile giving an oval frame to the face and there is a small self bow at the back below the crown. The whole is edged and swathed in black crêpe with black satin ribbons attached to the outside of the bonnet where the crown meets the brim.

Wedding Bonnets 1840s

Detail from an English fashion plate for December 1841, showing drawn bonnets.

Wedding dress has always involved substantial financial investment and the opportunity for a display of wealth and status. Although white was frequently worn prior to the 19th century, it was Queen Victoria's marriage to Prince Albert in 1840 that formalised the tradition for white as a symbol of purity and virginity. The 18th-century fashion for hats gave way to bridal wreaths, veils or veiled bonnets.

The first bonnet shown above right is made from silk tulle (a sheer and stiffened silk), tucked and ruched and decorated with rows of narrow cream silk ribbon applied in loops. It is partly shaped by stiffened white net and wired edges. The bonnet fits close to the head with ear pieces of heavily ruched and decorated tulle. It is trimmed with bows of the same silk ribbon and fastened with cream satin ribbons from the ear pieces, one with a ticket saying '3 yds' which may indicate it was a shop model.

Below right is a fine example of a drawn bonnet, a bonnet where the fabric covers a series of cane or whalebone hoops not dissimilar to the form of the calash (see pp.16 and 17). It was a style fashionable during this period. The cream silk bonnet curves in one line from a low crown over the top of the head to the edge of the brim, partly obscuring the profile. The sides curve down to meet under the chin giving a round frame to the face. The brim extends with silk net over a silk-covered wire frame and the matching bavolet is lined with net. There are ten supporting hoops of cane with three silk-covered wire struts supporting the crown. It is trimmed with a frill of silk gauze ribbon and tulle on a foundation of straw plait. The face is framed with a frill of cream silk lace around the outside edge of the brim and bavolet. It fastens with wide cream silk ribbon ties.

Hat Mid-19th century

At this period hats were considered only to be suitable for informal occasions such as a visit to the seaside or for countryside use. The *Illustrated London News* reported in 1855: 'The ladies are at present wearing a broad flapping starched hat of brown chip which overshadows their features like a huge parasol.'

This example is the epitome of the rural (and marine) idyll. It is a round hat with a low curved crown and a brim slightly dipping down all round. Made from thick whole straw plait it is completely covered with pine-cone scales. The crown is garlanded with real moss and seaweed on green woollen cord with a bow of acorn with acorn cup tassels. It is fastened with ribbed claret silk ribbon ties from the outside edge of the brim (possibly a later addition).

Bonnet 1850

This is an unusually modest bonnet of the time but of beautiful construction. It is made from narrow straw plait painted and stiffened to form a very hard and thick fabric. The vertical crown at the back of the head slopes slightly forward towards the top. The deep brim forms a circular frame to the face. The whole is lined with sapphire-blue silk and is decorated with wide sapphire-blue satin ribbon that forms a pleated and ruched band around the lower edge of the bonnet extending into long lappets. The back section of the pleating is held in place with a piece of red-painted card. Wide grey and green brocade ribbon ties pinned inside the brim fasten the bonnet.

Uglies 1848-1870

The ugly was a fashion item. The equivalent for working women was the sun bonnet, generally made from cotton with the crown stiffened with cord. This late 19th-century photograph shows Mary, a weeding woman, wearing a sun bonnet in the garden of Killerton House in Devon.

A new development in outdoor wear emerged to protect the complexion from the sun, known unprepossessingly as an ugly. The origin of the word seems to have derived from a comment made in *Punch* in 1848. It is constructed in a similar manner to the calash (see pp. 16 and 17) with fabric stretched over cane supports, but instead of covering the whole head it formed a detachable brim. This could be worn with the bonnet to give additional protection when the bonnet no longer shaded the face.

Many were made of silk or cotton stretched over cane hoops and fastened with ribbon ties.

56

Spoon Bonnet 1855-60

A wide array of affordable materials was now on offer. Increased industrialisation and better communication influenced the demand for cheaper materials. The invention of the sewing machine by Barthelemy Thimmonier, later perfected by Howe and Isaac Singer, encouraged more and more elaborate fashions and trimmings. Dress became fuller, first supported by layers of petticoats, then from the mid-1850s a hooped whalebone underskirt or the crinoline. This was a combination weave of crin (horsehair, already much used in millinery) and linen.

The effect on headwear was an increase in decoration. As Punch noted wryly in November 1861, 'The new fashionable spoon-shape of bonnets leaves a considerable space between the tip of the spoon and the organ of benevolence. This space is at present filled in with a dahlia or some other ornament.'

The spoon bonnet is characterised by the straight line from the crown to the brim with a sharp upward slant. The sides curve down to points at jaw level. This example is made from cream horsehair plait, hand-stitched through the overlapped plait in a spiral from the centre of the crown. It is lined with cream silk and has a bavolet of cream ribbed silk with heavy stiffened net. It is trimmed with black machine lace around the edge of the brim, the bavolet and across the centre of the bonnet. There is a cream ribbed silk ribbon bow on the left-hand side and a tiny plaited straw medallion with glass droppers in the centre of the bavolet. A frill of silk net and cream silk lace with flowers and leaves of grey-blue silk frame the face inside the brim and is pinned in place. The ties are missing.

58

Quaker Bonnet 1860

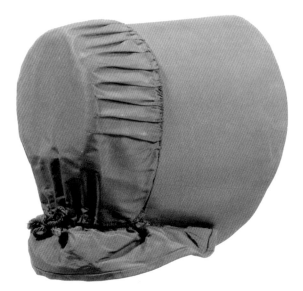

Some elements of headwear remained consistent through time; for example, that worn by the Quakers. This religious group, the Society of Friends, founded by George Fox in the mid-17th century, got its familiar name from his injunction to 'Tremble at the Word of the Lord'. In their dress the Quakers maintained a consistency of style and simplicity in keeping with their strict philosophical ideals. The unmistakable style, often known as Wagon, drew upon a subdued colour range of blacks and greys.

This black ribbed silk bonnet is made from a double layer of stiffened muslin with paper beneath. It has been steamed into shape with pleats around the curve of the crown. The card brim is edged with wire. The whole is covered with black ribbed silk and is lined with cream ribbed silk to the brim. The crown is formed from fabric gathered over card where it joins the brim and at the back above the bavolet. There is evidence of pins to hold ties inside the brim.

Fanchon Bonnet 1865-70

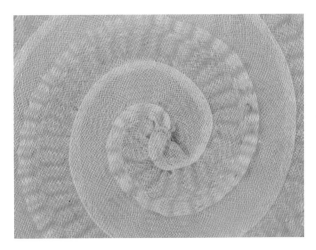

Detail from an English fashion plate showing a fanchon bonnet, July 1866.

The Fanchon bonnet (from the French for 'kerchief') was an innovation of Charlesworth, a Paris couturier. The *Ladies Treasury* of 1866 describes them as 'no longer bonnets but plaques of lace trimmed with the tiniest flowers'.

This winter fanchon bonnet was possibly made for a wedding. It is composed from alternating crimped and flat horsehair braids in cream, sewn in a spiral. The almost flat crown has narrow points over the ears and a wire frame. It has a band across the forehead and is lined with cream silk georgette. A circle of pleated cream satin ribbon edged with cream Bedfordshire Maltese lace decorates the hat. Cream roses and rosebuds frosted with glass beads and small mauve trumpet flowers also decorate the band and the right-hand side of the bonnet. There is a frill of tulle at the temples and the fastenings are of cream satin.

62

Fanchon Bonnet 1865-70

This shallow hat would have been worn placed towards the front of the head over a chignon. It curves down over the ears with a frill at the back of cream machine lace. and has a band across the forehead. It is made from pastel yellow satin and silk georgette in rows of box pleats across the bonnet with a wire frame and yellow georgette lining. It is edged with machine blonde-style lace with a satin ribbon bow centre front. The bar is decorated with cornflowers, poppies, daisies and ferns of coloured, stiffened cotton and feathers.

It is fastened with wide yellow satin ribbons that tie beneath the chignon. It also has long false ties of georgette and satin held with satin and lace bows at the throat and narrow ties of cream silk-fringed ribbon. Long ribbon streamers known as 'follow-me-lads' were a popular addition to hats and bonnets at this time.

64

Fanchon Bonnet 1860-1870

A bonnet of blue-black silk velvet and Venetian pink satin, with a shallow crown and narrow brim covered with satin. There is a velvet band over the forehead and a box-pleated bavolet of velvet faced with satin. Velvet and black machine lace form a loop and tail over the crown. The brim and forehead band are trimmed with pink cotton roses and rosebuds and russet leaves. There is cream machine lace on the forehead band. The ties are of dawn-pink ribbed silk with black velvet ribbon stripes.

Artificial flowers had become an essential ingredient of the milliner's art. C.T. Hinckley, writing in the *Ladies Companion* in 1854 describes workshops in France where these flowers were manufactured. Each workroom was equipped with long tables fitted with drawers and compartments containing the minute parts for assembly. A variety of textiles were used, including silk, gauze, velvet, muslin and cotton cambric, which were cut out in the shape of leaves and petals before being gauffered into shape.

Hat 1865-1870

Photograph of Lady Trevelyan of Wallington Hall, Northumberland, wearing an elaborate chignon.

The profile of dress was transformed during the 1860s, moving away from skirts that were circular to flat-fronted dresses with increasingly large bustles at the back. This profile was reflected in the fashionable hairstyle, the chignon, often a combination of real and false hair which could weigh up to five ounces. A style commentator pronounced in 1867, 'the smaller the bonnet, the larger the chignon'.

This hat is made from a straw plait overlapped and hand-stitched in a spiral from the centre of the crown. The whole has then been painted white. It is oval in shape with a shallow saucer-like crown and brim tipped down to fore and aft. The head lining has a printed trade-mark – a ship and hand holding ears of wheat. It is trimmed with honey ribbed silk ribbon and lilac satin ribbon with bows of the same. Black cotton machine-woven net over the top of the hat also hangs behind and the hat is decorated with two white and one yellow ostrich feathers. There was originally a narrow black elastic tie which would have gone under the chignon. A narrow velvet ribbon is pinned in place.

Hat 1865-70

This example is made from a straw plait, hand-stitched through overlapping plaits in a spiral from the crown centre. The hat is oval in shape with a shallow crown and a wired brim which is wider and tied down at the front and the back. It is trimmed with a band of twisted blue velvet ribbon and ribbed silk ribbon with a frill over the brim of black machine lace and cream silk lace. One blue ostrich feather decorates the crown. There is a blue ribbon bow and streamer with a wide streamer of black lace attached. The brim is faced with turquoise-blue ribbed silk.

Lace

Portrait of Anne Elizabeth Hood painted by Cyrus Johnson, at Dunster Castle in Somerset. The sitter is wearing a wealth of different kinds of lace, including a fanchon bonnet with lace lappets.

The lace industry was transformed by John Heathcoat's invention of the bobbin net machine, which he patented in 1809. Heathcoat originally had his factory in Loughborough in Leicestershire, but machine-breaking attacks obliged him to move his works and staff down to Tiverton in Devon, close to the hand lacemaking centre of Honiton.

Until Heathcoat's patent, lace was a highly luxurious commodity, available only to the wealthiest. Thereafter, it was available to a wide market. By the 1860s, a square yard of lace that would have cost £5 in 1810 could be purchased for 6d (2½p). Fortunately English manufactured lace was of high quality, and the industry was able to prosper because of the growing use of trimmings, particularly for wedding and mourning dress.

The two examples shown here are of black machine lace. Above: Detail from hat, 1865-70 (p.69)
Below: Detail from fanchon bonnet, 1860s (p.67)

72

Mourning Bonnet 1865-70

A bonnet for half-mourning (see p.48) made of violet satin, part quilted in squares with cream silk plush. It is flat with points over the ears and a band at the forehead. There is a point centre back with a deep frill of Bedfordshire Maltese lace. It is formed of stiffened cotton net overlaying a wire frame. Violet satin frills decorate the edge and a bow of satin edged with plush the centre. The band is criss-crossed with violet satin and there is a frill of tulle at the temples. It is fastened with cream satin ribbons and has hanging ties of violet satin pinned together with a satin ribbon bow.

Hat 1870

Even amongst the working classes there was a great variety in shape and trimmings of hats, as seen in this late 19th-century photograph of a group of hop pickers in Kent.

Amongst the fashionable, many styles of hat became popular, such as the bergère (as seen in the 18th century, see pp.6-14), the sailor hat (made popular by the Prince of Wales), the Tyrolese (which resembled an inverted flower-pot) and small straw hats with flower pot crowns and narrow brims.

This small round hat was designed to perch on top of the hair at a slightly tilted angle. It has a high crown and small brim made of stiffened net covered with string-coloured grosgrain pleated and looped with a bow and streamers at the back. The brim is edged with wire. The head and side are lined separately with cream silk

and it is trimmed with a band of pleated Neyron rose satin ribbon on the underside of the brim with country flowers at the front. These are stiffened cotton and satin cornflowers and poppies with ears of wheat made from folded paper and horsehair. Two cream ostrich feathers provide extra decoration. The streamers have a grey silk fringe and there are narrow black elastic ties with a jet button weight.

Hat 1870

James Tissot's, The Crack Shot, painted c. 1870 showing a fashionably dressed lady with her hat perched on her chignon.

The enormous variety of trimmings available at this period ranged from 'worm-eaten faded green leaves' to feathers and whole stuffed birds. Nature provided what appeared to be an inexhaustible resource of the latter. A single consignment of birds from South America might contain 40,000 humming birds to provide aigrettes for millinery. One writer in 1875 declared that the beauty of these birds 'tempts the most tender hearted to condone the cruelty by which they are obtained', but not everybody condoned the practice. It was reckoned in 1895 that 'some twenty to thirty million dead birds are imported into this country annually to supply the demands of murderous millinery'. Such excesses galvanised a group of ladies from Manchester to form the Fur, Fin and Feather Group in 1889. This later became the Royal Society for the Protection of Birds.

The hat shown here is of a nettle-grey silk velour on a cotton ground over a double layer of sized buckram. It is oval with a shallow crown and a brim all around, wider and tilted downwards back and front. It has black machine lace at the back and it is lined with black taffeta. A band and bow of velour edged with black lace decorates the hat with a pink ostrich feather around the sides and the back. There are the remains of a black elastic tape which would have secured the hat under the chignon.

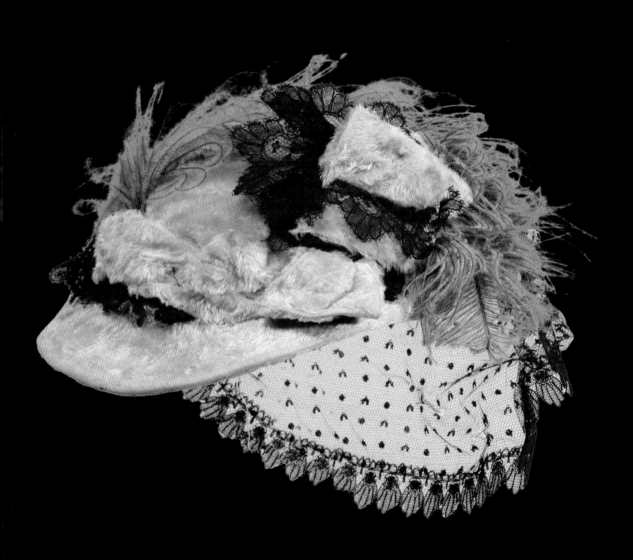

Hat Late 1870s

Margaret, Lady Verney of Claydon House in Oxfordshire, a portrait by William Blake Richmond painted in 1869. She is depicted carrying her feathered straw hat.

A natural leghorn straw hat. The crown is lined with cream silk with a narrow cotton draw tape with silk head lining beneath. The brim is faced with georgette tucked in wavy lines. It has a shallow, round, straight-sided crown with a brim all round widening at the front. The back is fluted and the edge of an originally round brim is wired and folds under. It is trimmed with a wide band of loosely pleated georgette at the back of the hat, the folds held out with two pieces of wire. A large cream silk bow sits centre front.

There is a narrow black elastic tape loop, now perished, which would have been worn under the chignon.

This hat looks deceptively large. The diameter is in fact 31.75cms/12½ ins.

Mourning Hat 1870s

Fashion plate from Le Monde Elégant for April 1867 showing a similar hat.

A mourning hat of moulded leghorn straw. It is fully lined with black taffeta and has an oval shape with a shallow crown. There is a brim all around, wider at the front and back. The boater shape tilted down front and back was particularly popular. The trimmings are of black satin with bows of black velvet, black machine-embroidered net and black ostrich feathers at the back. There is evidence of narrow black elastic inside.

Retailers responded energetically to the Victorian obsession with death. By the 1860s London's Regent Street offered several mourning warehouses, where all the garments and trimmings required for funerals and the aftermath were for sale. Peter Robinson not only had an extensive shop in Oxford Street, but in 1865 opened his 'Court and General Mourning House' at 262-65 Regent Street which was devoted entirely to the 'apparel and apparatus of grief'. He became known as Black Peter Robinson.

As etiquette dictated that widows and bereaved daughters should not be seen out of doors before the funeral, Black Peter Robinson and his rivals would go to them. He kept a carriage prepared with a coachman all in black. Two lady fitters, also in black, sat in the brougham equipped with patterns and designs, ready to dash through the London streets to attend the mourning household and rush through the order for their outfits.

Straw Hats Late 19th century

The example on the right is a natural fine straw hat made from a 7-end plait. It has been hand-stitched and sold in its untrimmed state ready for trimming at home. The crown and the brim have been made separately and subsequently joined. It has a small, high sloping crown with a narrow slanting brim and is designed to sit on top of the head. There is a ticket on the outside for four shillings 'London'.

Another fine example of a hand-stitched straw hat, above, seen as sold before being trimmed. It is made from a 7-end plait and has a cream sateen lining. The head lining is printed with the maker's mark, a globe and coat of arms and 'London Manufacture'. This example has a deep crown with slanting sides, a narrow brim with a slight curl at the edge. There is a price label on the outside of the brim.

By the 1880s manufacture of straw hats was focussed in particular towns like Luton in Bedfordshire. Milliners throughout the country would be supplied with basic forms for trimming or selling on to customers to trim at home.

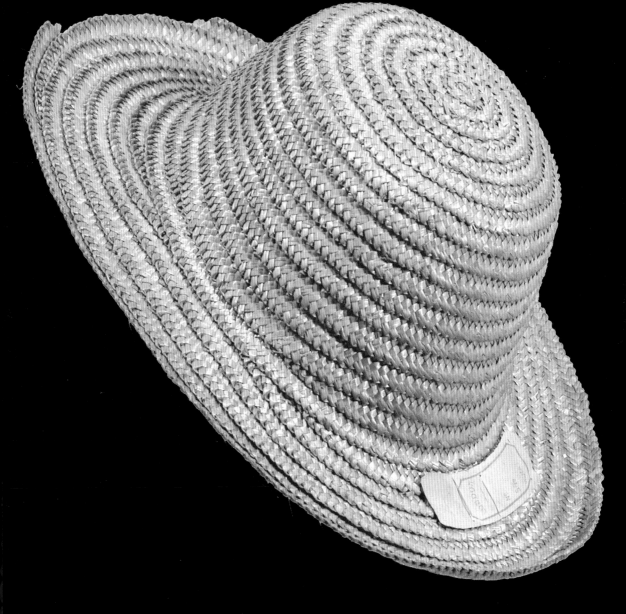

Bonnet 1885-90

English fashion plate for August 1888, showing how bonnets and hats were worn perched on the top of the head.

A bonnet made from natural cream horsehair with raised Vandyke points at the edge. It is hand-stitched through overlapped braid in a spiral from the centre of the crown. The crown is shallow and oval shaped, with the front side slanting upwards and a narrow brim at a sharp angle to the crown, the underside perpendicular centre front. It is designed to perch on the top of the head. The crown and brim are made in one piece and the edge wired.

The bonnet is fully lined with cream silk with separate crown, side and head linings. The head lining is printed with the maker's name in gold 'James ?Cubison 188 Oxford Street, London'. It is trimmed with maroon silk velvet inside the brim and edged with gold-coloured metal braid. The outside trim is missing.

86

Bonnet 1885-90

A bonnet of natural cream horsehair hand-stitched through overlapped plait in a spiral from the centre of the crown. The crown has a shallow oval shape tilted upwards with a narrow, sharply upturned brim around the front only. It was designed to perch over the hair on top of the head. The edge is wired and the brim is stitched to the crown. It is lined with double silk tulle gathered at the centre of the crown. It has a cream crimped tulle bavolet with ruched tulle at the front of the brim. The inside of the brim is edged with gold-coloured metal thread, the outside of the brim and the top of the bavolet are edged with swansdown.

Straw Hat Late 19th century

English fashion plate showing the style of hats and hairstyles for 1891.

A hat of novelty straw braid, hand sewn in a spiral. The oval shallow crown has a flat brim all round with a wired edge. The crown is lined with cream sateen with a pinned trademark of a globe with coat of arms, indicating London manufacture. It is trimmed with narrow black lace inside the edge of the brim with a garland of silk tulle and sprays of small white cotton flowers, glazed cotton leaves and stems with glass drops.

This hat is tiny, only 22cms/ 8$\frac{1}{4}$ ins across at its greatest width, and intended to perch on the top of the head.

90

Straw Boater *c.*1900

The daughters of the Prince and Princess of Wales with an unknown companion exploring the estate at Cragside in Northumberland during their royal visit in 1884. The watercolourist H.H. Emmerson has shown the royal trio wearing straw boaters.

A style that became very popular for ladies at the end of the 19th century was the straw boater, adapted from the 'Henley Boater' which was originally a felt boater-shaped hat worn by men. It remained in fashion until the 1930s, often for outdoor activities such as punting and cycling, and its popularity prompted the comment 'as women have taken to straw boaters, it seems almost effeminacy for a mere man to don anything of the kind'. After 1930 it became standard uniform for schoolchildren of both sexes, and for tradesmen. This example is typical in shape, with checked, double split, 6-end plait straw heavily stiffened with shellac and hand-stitched.

Glossary

BAVOLET the back ruffle or curtain on a bonnet

BOATER a stiff oval straw hat coated with shellac, fashionable from the end of the 19th century

BONNET a soft head covering with ties

BUCKRAM a fine linen or cotton fabric stiffened with gum or paste

CALASH, CALÈCHE a large collapsible hood named after the French carriage – calèche

CAP a brimless headdress worn for various occasions through the day

CHIGNON a large knot of hair worn at the back of the head. Popular at various times. During the 19th century it often weighed 5 ounces (150g)

COTTAGE BONNET a straw bonnet with a brim projecting beyond the cheeks. Popular from 1808, it was modified during the century, the brim being lined and rolled backwards

DEVONSHIRE HAT a very large, wide-brimmed hat, generally trimmed, with a deep crown. Made popular by Thomas Gainsborough's portrait of Georgiana, Duchess of Devonshire. Also known as 'picture hat'. The style reappeared in the late 19th century

DORMEUSE indoor or night-time (dormouse) cap of muslin, lawn or linen, fitting loosely over the coiffure

ELASTIC cord, thread or string woven with india-rubber. Invented in 1820 by an Englishman, T. Hancock

FANCHON small, lace-edged kerchief used as head-dressing or trimming over the ears of a day bonnet from 1830s

FANCHON CAP lace or tulle bonnet with deep ruffle at the back of the head from 1840s

FLORENTINE HAT made from fine straw from Tuscany, cut green and bleached

GROSGRAIN hard-wearing corded silk fabric

LAPPETS pieces of fabric or pairs of pendant strips made of ribbon, fabric or lace hanging from the head-covering, bonnet or gable hood

LUNARDI HAT a large hat with a crown of puffed gauze, named after Vincenzi Lunardi, who made the first manned flight in a balloon in Great Britain in 1784

PAMELA BONNET straw trimmed with flowers on a sloping brim tied with ribbons, named in 1845 after Samuel Richardson's 18th-century eponymous heroine Pamela

POKE BONNET late 18th-century, early 19th-century bonnet with coal-scuttle shaped brim protruding over the face, first worn over the cap and with ribbon ties

QUAKER BONNET also known as the Wagon Bonnet from its resemblance to a covered wagon

SPOON BONNET narrow brim at the sides rising high above the face in a spoon-shaped curve, sloping down at the back and edged with a bavolet, 1860s

TULLE fine silk net originally from Tulle, France

UGLY folding brim worn in front of a bonnet for protection against the sun, from 1848

Picture Credits

First published in Great Britain in 2004 by
National Trust Enterprises Limited
36 Queen Anne's Gate
London SW1H 9AS

www.nationaltrust.org.uk

ISBN 0 7078 0384 5

Designed by SMITH

Editorial and picture research by Margaret Willes
Colour origination by Digital Imaging Ltd. Glasgow
Printed in China by WKT Co. Ltd.

Cover: Bergère, 1750s (see pp.6 and 7)
Half title: Bergère, 1750-70 (see pp.12 and 13)
Frontispiece: Mid-19th-century hat (see pp.52 and 53)
Title: Bonnet, late 1820s (see pp.26 and 27)